Advance Praise for
Prospect When You Are Happy

"Even seasoned professionals can tend to lose sight of the importance of attitude. This book will re-awaken those fundamentals.
Erica Nelson did a great job of setting the tone of being happy,
right from the start, and keeping that mindset at the forefront
throughout. Erica has successfully demonstrated that a happy
attitude will dictate positive thinking, confidence, and positive
results. Nice job!"
    ~ CarGuyMike, Mike Feller, Innovative Sales & Leasing

"I love this book. It has great examples and tools to help improve
your mood and thus prospecting potential. I had great fun setting
my intentions and now I am excited to see how all the fabulous
things I have stated show up in my life. Anyone who wants to live
their best life and have fun along the way must read this book, it is
GOLD!"
    ~ Suzanne Nicholas, Independent Distributor, Xocai

"This is an incredibly insightful book with amazing, easy and
practical applications. Law of Attraction must be put into action
to work. It is not sitting on a couch - not doing anything. This
book will give you the infusion of inspiration that you need and
prime you to get Law of Attraction working for you...a must read
if you ever prospect."
    ~ Michelle Humphrey, Founder and CEO, Effortless Living
        Institute, Co-Star of "Pass It On"

"I always stop and get into a good mood before I call a client.
Working with Erica has taught me the importance of prospecting
when I am happy. I have tried prospecting when I am miserable.
The phone weighs, oh about 1000 pounds, walking to someone's
door is like climbing Mount Everest, typing a simple email can
take an hour. Not to mention that when I do that I am not successful. When I am happy the words flow out of my mouth, I know
exactly the right thing to say to get the clients that I want. And
most importantly I have fun."
    ~ Maria Kellis, Keller Williams Realty

"I sincerely loved this book! It was fun to read, it was uplifting, and it's full of great practical tools to bring success to one's life in general. This is a truly inspiring book about how to very effectively use the power of love and attraction to achieve big success in your life. I felt increasingly empowered, self-confident, and happy about my potential as I read each page, and I've seen significant results from using the techniques Erica describes. Thank you for this gift of wisdom!"

~ Walter Zajac, PsychicWalter.com

"With every chapter I thought about different clients that would benefit from reading this book. Then I laughed out loud because every client showed up at some point, even those not remotely interested in sales! This is an easy to read, simple to implement, practical primer for creating the life you want. It will become 'assigned reading' for all of my clients."

~ Celeste Hamman, Health and Happiness Life Coach

Prospect When You Are Happy

Prospect When You Are Happy

Move the Law of Attraction into Action

ERICA M. NELSON

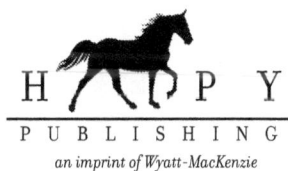

H P Y

PUBLISHING

an imprint of Wyatt-MacKenzie

Prospect When You Are Happy
Move the Law of Attraction into Action
by Erica M. Nelson

FIRST   EDITION

ISBN: 978-1932279-81-8

Library of Congress Control Number: 2007939625

H 🐎 P Y
PUBLISHING
an imprint of Wyatt-MacKenzie

Wyatt-MacKenzie Publishing, Inc.,
Deadwood, OR
www.WyMacPublishing.com
(541) 964-3314

Printed in the United States of America.

TABLE OF CONTENTS

Introduction

When I look back on my successful, albeit brief, venture into a real estate career, I realize the deals came to me when I was riding my horse, playing with my children and when I was feeling relaxed, happy and good about my life.

In 2004, I broke into the market as a realtor with zest and excitement. It was a major career change because for most of my professional life, I wrote. Newsrooms were my home. I wrote for California newspapers for more than a decade, before I transitioned to writing for public television. Selling had never occurred to me, until I had small children and wanted autonomy for my day-to-day environment.

I took a home listing to sell the day I obtained my real estate license. I sold about a house a month for the first 18 or 19 months in business. This was in California's Silicon Valley, where most houses sell for $600,000 to $900,000. The market climate was warm.

Within a year, realtors were clamoring to learn my system. How was I succeeding? Why was I so lucky? Meanwhile, the national consciousness was waking up to the fundamental concept of the Law of Attraction. This was a concept I had always understood.

As I looked on the landscape of the national consciousness, I became firmly re-acquainted with my own beliefs and practices on how to focus your energy to create your own success. This book is an answer to questions from students I began to coach and teach on the concept of the Law of Attraction: how to be aware that you create your reality. Students came to me to learn this. I had always lived with the awareness of the ability to focus your eyes on the prize to achieve positive change.

I began mentoring realtors at Keller Williams Realty in Cupertino, California. Soon I was teaching, coaching or mentoring realtors across a dozen real estate companies.

As I focused on helping people, I realized that the gift of a positive mindset was the greatest gift I could share with my students — not the information around "how to be a realtor," where thousands of people would be more qualified to teach than I. What people really wanted from me was the inspiration to generate sales results with confidence and competence.

This book was born on a camping trip in July 2007. I woke up on 40 acres my husband and I bought in the Santa Cruz Mountains and the title flashed in my head. All the chapter titles arrived the same way. I scrambled for pen and paper in our messy Yukon XL packed with clothing, paper towels, juice boxes and snacks for our trio of children who were 4, 5 and 6 years old at the time.

In the months before this book was conceived, I was teaching and coaching people in various sales positions — network marketing, merchant services, real estate — plus moms who were seeking a way to be more at peace and to experience more prosperity without losing the integrity of being a mom. So I had two businesses cooking: coaching business people and coaching moms.

Students, this book is for you! Friends, this book is for you!

This book is here to light you up, to get you going, and nudge you on your path. You may read it front to back or open to any page you like at any time. You may read passages again and again, or you may read it one time and let it go. Some chapters may be more meaningful than others. Trust your inner knowing. Pick up the book to get you into a good place. Be in a good place when you seek business. Be in a good mood when you call people. Trust the success that exists within you.

One book that changed my life was "The Dancing Wu Li Masters," by Gary Zukov. The physics illustrated in the book contend that when you walk into a room, your particles change whatever is in the room. The observer changes the observed. The evidence behind what my book is about can be found in that book.

Get into a good mood more often. You can. You can change your chemical reactions. You can change how you respond to people and how you give your energy to others. You can change where you are going, and you can change what you believe about where you have been.

I wrote this book to share the gift of seeing the glass "half-full." Fortunately, this is my birthright. I am an eternal optimist. I see the light in everyone. I look at people and see the smile way beneath the surface.

What happens when you see light and good in every single human being is that you charm and delight people without effort. Then you can do your business or run your life from a place of great support, continuity, and trust that everything is happening for the greater good of mankind.

I have had great help. Look for the pages at the end of the story, where I will acknowledge some of the people whose light guided me on this journey.

Enjoy the book! Share with friends! I wrote this book with joy to share how we can all achieve more, every day. Prospect when you are happy! It works.

"My Father is in the Printing business, but this is ridiculous"

In this chapter, you will learn:

• *An overview of the book: what to expect when you prospect when you are happy*
• *Why prospecting from an excited, motivated and focused point of view will bring you more results*

CHAPTER 1

Prospect When You Are Happy

When was the last time you saw a breathtaking double rainbow arc across the sky? Dolphins swimming in the ocean, leaping with joy? Can you bring into your mind the moment of your child's first smile? When a loved one gave you a hug? How did it feel to deposit the largest check you have ever held in your hands? To drive off the lot in a brand new car?

Do you realize you can live any lifestyle you choose? You have the key to your future. You dictate the shape of the key and the size of your house, the color of your car, the way your friends and family smile and create warmth around you — all of this is at your command. Be in the driver's seat. Focus where you choose to focus. Encourage the aspects of yourself you wish to encourage.

Be a person who is committed to discovering how you can shine, every day.

When a dream or a vision strikes a chord within your being — and you begin to see that vision become your life — you have at your fingertips all that you need to make that vision come true. When you allow your energy to naturally flow through you, the vision leads to inspired action. And that action will then bring everything you want into your life.

On these pages, you will find the tools to enable you to create more wealth, finer results, and obtain greater return on your investment of energy every day. This book is a sales primer with an infusion of inspiration. Why not improve the result of every call? Why not inspire the communication with every person you meet? Are sales coming to you easily? Are you achieving what you want in your life? Allow these pages to take you step by step through a practical re-alignment of vision, into a place where results come to you with rapid-fire speed.

Believe in who you are and what you bring, believe in your service or your product, and be in a good place when you present information about it. These pages will guide you through steps that will lift your results off the map. Begin with a smile, and if you are not feeling good, take action so that you can smile before you make a call or communicate about your product or service.

The Law of Attraction states that like attracts like. To attract amazing clients and wonderful business partners, become that which you wish to behold.

You're going to learn how your energy emits waves like a radio tower. And how people are drawn to the light you project.

As you become clear on your intention, you will begin to experience stronger results. Focused intention is a rare find. People often go about their day distracted, listening to scraps of conversations here and there, pondering where they will be in a few minutes. It is so easy to become bogged down in thoughts that do not assist in getting the results you wish to experience.

Get to know exactly what you want. Then beam that out. Clarity of intent is a gift you can give — and others will respond with amazing speed.

When I teach groups about getting into a good place — feeling that sense of power, joy, inspiration, happiness…all those wonderful feelings that can brim out of your being — I then ask "How can *you* do that? How can *you* feel happy before

Change your energy if you don't like your energy. Become that person to whom people flock in any room or crowd.

Become so attractive, by the beaming smile on your face, that people who don't even know what you are about want to be part of whatever you are doing.

you prospect?" Everyone looks to *me* for the answer.

The funny thing is that the teacher really doesn't know how you can find the happiness for you, within you. *You* possess your own set of chemical reactions. You know what makes you dance inside, how to feel powerful, what moves you to tears? Every individual on the planet has a different set of wires and connections that create his or her being. Your individual path to happiness, freedom, joy and exuberance comes from within.

Here you will find practical steps to put you in touch with that sense of happiness within. You will find a list of suggested activities, and instructions for taking gentle steps to lead you into your own bliss. Why not feel good before you do anything?

Today we are in a time where immediate communication with people prevails. We will look at skills for getting into your own energy and making sure that cell phones, e-mails, texting and other means of touching another person's space can be navigated while keeping your own sense of self intact.

Sales people so often believe that they need to be immediately present for a client. The client may express this need. However, what he or she truly may want at a deeper level is to connect with that powerful, positive, sure and amazing individual he or she met in the beginning. So if the phone rings at the wrong time for you, this book will empower you to stay in your own chemistry prior to communicating. In this way, you may find that others no longer have the power to shift or change your energy.

We will walk through what happens when you don't clear your energy and stay in a good place prior to connecting with people. What will you give up if you do not dedicate yourself to the positive future you can create? What do you risk?

When you operate at a lower level of success, you may fail to achieve your intentions. Is this what you want? Look at the risks associated with resisting change. For example, if you wish to be in health, and you weigh way too much, you may risk heart disease if you decline opportunities to shift your energy and embrace health. If you wish wealth, and you decline opportunities that can move you into a better financial situation, you risk losing the wealth that you desire.

If you don't change, you will stay the same. That sounds so simple. When you keep the same thought patterns, it is extremely difficult to effect measurable change in your life. When you change your thoughts and become connected to the brightness within your spirit, change happens without so much effort. Unless you resist.

Getting into a good place will improve your results. When you slip into someone else's negative energy or succumb to your own, this lowers your personal outcomes. These pages will show you how to turn your energy around and keep navigating to your vision.

Then when you feel really good, clear and happy, and you are focused on victory, you will learn secrets about attracting perfect clients. Who is your perfect client? Someone who wants your services? Someone appreciative and generous? Are you drawn to big thinkers? Imagine, for a moment, how you will feel when your perfect client walks into your life.

Just because something swerved into the road and you pulled aside for a few minutes, it does not mean you cannot focus on getting back to driving where you want to go.

Now you are brimming with success, perfect clients are flocking to you like bees to honey, and you can dream large again. Clarify your intention; get more into your dream. Become happy knowing that you have the power to create the fabric of your life.

Become one with double rainbows that arc across the sky. Be triumphant with the soaring eagle that can see the earth below. Feel the power of your own solid bank account, financial security, retirement. Experience the power to own what you want to own. Give yourself your energy back. Own it; be true to your own energy.

Then, prospect when you are happy. It works.

What this chapter will teach:

· *How your energy beams out and influences the result of your efforts*

· *How to get into a good place before you make the call, then watch your results skyrocket*

CHAPTER 2

Smile When You Make the Call

Beam a huge smile before you make a call. Drive to a sales appointment with complete commitment to an outstanding experience. Your thoughts are powerful signals. As you send powerfully joyful, happy, relaxed, confident, intense and service-oriented thoughts, people will not be able to say no to your product or service — unless they have no need for it at all.

Your product or service will be in greater demand when you present it from a positive state of being. You — the conduit for the service — feel good about everything you do. You feel strong, delighted, interested and caring about the quality of the service you provide.

No doubt you have personally experienced the opposite. Think about walking into a restaurant and having a grumpy, tired, harried and half-asleep person taking your order.

As human beings, we strive to be in harmony with each other at an energetic level. So the half-asleep waiter who is not paying attention to your order likely may make mistakes, and compound this negative mindset with negative outcomes, perhaps bringing you the wrong thing or forgetting half of what he or she was supposed to bring.

Change it around. Walk in and ask for a different server if yours appears to be in a bad mood. Or go to a different restaurant. Or joke and play with the grumpy person until he or she can't help but smile, laugh and cheer up. This smiling person can now take your order with a better level of competence — his or her mood has shifted.

In the moment you are communicating your product or service, who are you? Are you tired? Convinced it won't work and you will have to make 65 more calls to get one appointment? What are you thinking about when you are picking up the phone? Are you focused on the communication at hand, or are you in 30 other places figuring out what you are going to do next, when you are going to get time to take the dog to the vet, or thinking about the bills you have to pay?

As you drive to a sales appointment, your thoughts already are moving into place to shift the energy of the outcome of that appointment. You are a radio tower, and your signals are sending out thoughts and feelings all of the time. When you are feeling *good*, these thoughts and feelings fly on wings and all of the energy in the room shifts to make room for your intense feelings of joy, happiness and peace. No one can take that from you, ever.

You have choices. When you are clear and bright with your own energy, you will attract high-level people whom you are likely to enjoy immensely in your life. You can change energy in a room, change the energy in a dialog, and change the energy of a relationship.

As you refine this way of being — and become clearer and clearer about staying present to your own peace, joy and enthusiasm — what occurs is that the whole universe shifts and brings you people who are enjoyable to be around. You may develop excellent radar that will show you when it is right to go into business with another person, or when it wrong. You have permission to say no and cut your losses.

When you prospect from a place of happiness and calm security, people don't really care what you are selling; they are attracted to you and want to be near you. If you are selling real estate, they will send you real estate clients and opportunities. If you are selling face-cream products in a network marketing capacity, they will send you people who want to sign up with you to sell face-cream products. It's about being a high-energy, fantastic individual. Then no one can stop you from achieving what you wish to achieve.

Much is said about choosing a block of time each day and going through scripts, cold-calling lists of potential clients, and spending several hours each day contacting dozens of individuals to pitch your product. When you focus your intention more brightly, and refine your energy so that it beams with intensity, you will experience more fun with your calls and greater results with every communication. If you stay in an automatic or less-than-intense state of being, watch the return on your energy investment decrease. The more you allow yourself to become, the more you will be able to attract people to your vision with ease.

One time I was taking a class on building your business at a real estate company. An experienced realtor shared the value of cold calling. She talked about how she had to make 700 contacts to achieve 20 listing appointments to sell two houses. "It's a numbers game" — the more calls you make, the more appointments you get, the greater number of sales you can close, she told the audience.

Wouldn't it be more fun if you could influence the ratio of calls-to-appointments-to-sales? Perhaps, in the situation of the realtor, with focused intensity and positive intention while prospecting, he or she could make 30 or 40 calls, set two or three appointments and then sell those homes. Now, would that be more fun?

Or what if you never made a cold call? You woke up and set your intention. Then you contacted people who you know, who could lead you to the results you are seeking. Perhaps you become inspired to go to a festival or event, and meet people who connect you to the right business opportunities. Being in the flow means the results show up. When you are clear on what you want, and this wish will be of service to you and to the planet, the results flow into your life.

When you approach each call, each appointment, and each potential sale as a golden winning opportunity, you have a different way about you. As you close and close and close, you become known as what? A Closer. Wouldn't that be great? Wouldn't that make you smile?

The tools applied herein have the potential to powerfully increase your results. As you begin to read the energy of people around you, you won't spend so much time forcing ill-fitting transactions into place. As you begin to read energy, you will find yourself able to give excellent service and match yourself with clients who want everything that you want.

For one moment in time — right now — suspend all negative thoughts about any past performance. Commit, in this moment, for today, to being present, focused, clear, and in a good place for each and every client interaction in the next 10 days. Try it. See what happens.

Later in this book we talk about getting clear on your perfect client. You'll be asked to begin to figure out what that perfect client is like. As you get clear on your perfect client, and increase your desire to meet people with certain characteristics, you will attract people with these qualities that you seek. How wonderful would that feel? If through those lists of people and prospects that you sift through, you could identify those that will emerge as your perfect clients, wouldn't that be great?

This now may sound Pie-in-The-Sky. It's not. People who are tuned in to energy can sift and sort through lists of people and pre-select winning connections. That may not be possible for you at this time, but it is exciting to know that it works for some people. You've met them. They are so lucky! They land on their feet! Perfect clients show up for them at the oddest moments. Like the lucky salesperson who lands a transaction from the taxi driver who drives him or her home from the airport. Or the person who meets clients standing in line at the grocery store and closes 20 transactions from one "chance" meeting. This is all possible, should you choose to prospect when you are happy.

What you will learn in this chapter:

• *How to change your intention, then experience greater outcomes*

• *To focus on improving what you expect from every situation*

CHAPTER 3

Setting Your Intention

Before we go into how to always be in a good place when you prospect, it may help to understand your own power to set intention for all of your experiences. You can begin to realize how the process of setting the intention shapes the outcome of each of your experiences.

One student of mine could not believe how the process of setting an intention could change her life so quickly. She left a one-hour class on this topic and became very clear that she wanted referrals for her business. I'll call her AK. AK then went about her work for the week. She kept thinking about how wonderful referrals would feel, and how she felt when people gave them to her.

We were in class on Mondays. She came to the second class. Students were invited to share good experiences from the previous week. "Well, I picked up six referrals," AK said. SIX?! The rest of the class was in awe. Yes, four from one client, in fact, and two from another. "I couldn't believe that in one hour of class I could change so much," said AK. She had never really thought about having intention around her experiences.

Let's go back to the winter of 1988, and I am writing for a small daily newspaper in Lake Tahoe, California. I am on a mission to work for the Sacramento Bee and I am writing stories about casinos, entertainers, schools and county government. I don't have a bad job, but it is my intention to work for the Bee.

I find out about an opening at the Sacramento Bee for a junior reporter. I write one resume. I mail it to the right person. Then, I call the Bee and say I am going to be in the Sacramento area on a certain day, would it be convenient if I came by to say hello?

This pattern of setting intention works. I set the intention to write for the Sacramento Bee when I was 24 years old. I met with the publisher of that newspaper and listened to everything he suggested. I got some small newspaper experience, was fortunate to win some awards, and landed a job at my dream newspaper when I was 26. When the Sacramento Bee hired me, it was one of those exciting moments where I could not believe my good fortune. It became a habit for me to become clear on what I wanted and then write one resume strategically designed for the one job that I wanted.

As you become clear on your intended outcomes from your energy expenditures, your results have the potential to shift upwards. Let's say you wish to contact five businesses about your company. Remember: Get yourself in a really good place before contacting the first business. Get a clear picture of the outcome you want to occur. Take the time to think it through. Let's say you sell credit card processing equipment and services. And you are about to call a dentist's office.

Picture a very nice person who also happens to be the office accountant answering the phone. Picture he or she has been thinking about changing their credit card service and this person is so happy you called. In fact, he or she has time to meet with you the next morning if you want to come over and tell them how they can do a better job with check conversion and show them how to save money on each credit card sale. Then picture this! The accountant is a leader on a group of accountants networked nationally to achieve best practices, and would be happy to get you in front of her group of 100 other accountants.

When you set intentions, it is a great idea to just ask "what would be great," and then think about something even better. Now before you make that call, how are you feeling? Excited? Anticipating something good? Wondering if so many referrals will fall into your lap you won't know how to manage them all?

Most people would enjoy that problem.

Now you make the call. Oh no! No one is available to speak with you right now. Let it go. Get clear again on your intention. Beam it out. Then, gently look down the list of people you planned to contact that day. Does anyone stand out? Do any seem more inviting than others? For a moment, hold back any doubts of your own ability to do this practice and call the first person who comes to mind.

Set your intention again, and get back into a good place. This works for sales appointments, open houses (if you are a realtor), job interviews, and many other opportunities where you are pitching something to someone and you have a desire to experience a certain outcome.

What if nothing happens? Here is the problem with that question. How do you *know* nothing happened? How can you be CERTAIN that nothing happened?

What happens if you leave the most amazingly inspiring voice mail message? Let's go back to the example of the potential sale to the dentist. In your message, you say that you can't wait to share with the accountant how well your products will work for them.

Oh my. The accountant is on vacation. Two weeks go by. Then, your phone rings. Imagine the accountant so liked your voice mail that in sorting through all of the inbox items that built up over several weeks, she calls you back and you get into a great dialog.

The human mind tends to run with the negative. So we could, as human beings, deduce from the fact that we did not make an actual sale, close and earn a commission ON THE MOMENT OF THE FIRST CALL, that in fact we are terrible sales people and cannot ever do anything right. We can go into a huge tailspin and be convinced of our failure.

What if, instead, you remain certain that wonderful outcomes will happen? The right people will come into your life, and the right things will happen so that you can achieve all of your goals. Try this. For a few weeks, believe in the absolute perfection of the universe. That we are always being matched with people and places whose energy matches our own.

When you come from a place of complete confidence and security, the sales will fall into place. Be completely assured that this is working, far before the evidence falls into place.

How to Set an Intention

You may wish to write your intentions for your year, your month, your week and your days. Once you have become extremely clear on your intention, let it go and go about your business.

For example, you may have goals you wish to achieve within a year.

Writing them down infuses the vision with the strongest ability for it to become reality. Hint: Write in the present future tense. For example:

> In December, 200_, I am driving a convertible BMW
> (or name your car of dreams).

> In December, 200_, I am attracting $10,000 per week
> in residual income.

Name it, say it and begin to feel the results of getting to that goal or desire.

Once you have spent some time getting clear on where you want to be a year from now, take some time to become clear on the outcomes you want to experience a month from now.

Write at least 10 things that would be great to have in your life one month from today. For example:

> In December, 200_, I am waking up motivated every
> day. I love my career.

> In December, 200_, my daughter is reading with
> ease.

You can think up things that are work-related, sales-related, family-related, and health-related. Just about anything that you can think of, you can dream about and set into motion.

What stops you from setting a clear intention?

You may have reached this point in the book and you may be afraid to write down your intentions. Or maybe you feel too busy to stop and write them down.

Let's just say that you now have permission to:

• write mistaken intentions

• write intentions that aren't good enough

• write intentions that later you may laugh about

• write intentions that have a .002 percent chance of coming true in your present mindset

• write your dream intentions

• write small intentions that you are 100 percent certain will happen

• write intentions for things like finding a parking place or driving safely to your appointments

• write intentions for experiencing more of what you want without knowing exactly what that may look or feel like

As you work backwards from the future to the present, you begin to infuse your intention into every waking moment. Your intention begins to beam out from you — and this vision is something that will allow people to fall into alignment around you.

Let go of your fears around declaring your wishes, your dreams, your vision. When you let go of your fears and move into calm expectation of great results, your vision can become reality. Can it be that simple?

Once I was listening to a wildly popular musician and songwriter talking about how she wrote music and her advice was amazing. She said that she gives herself permission to write really bad music. She allows herself to write lyrics that no one would ever sing! Once she gets over that block of everything needing to be perfect before she writes, then the words and music flow.

If you have not already done so, please stop everything you are doing right now and write down at least three intentions for a year from now. Then write at least three intentions for a month from now. And now for the greatest challenge: Stop and think about your day today (or tomorrow if it is very late) and write three intentions for today or tomorrow.

What Next?

Here is one excerpt from a student who took the time to write her intentions:

Dear Erica,

By the way, I am still on target to run 1,000 miles for this year. I have only been able to accomplish this goal once in my life, and that was back in 2003. I never imagined that I would be able to do it again, especially with two little boys, but thanks to the letter that you asked me to write to myself, it truly has been effortless. I get out to run five times a week, and I never think twice about it. Some times, the only way that I can get out is if I take my boys with me, and I have discovered that they enjoy the run just as much as I do.

Thank you for giving me this wonderful opportunity, Erica!

— Sonia (Cupertino, CA)

Once you have taken the time to write your intentions, you will be amazed at how many good things begin to occur. This very action of writing causes change. In fact, you need to do very little else. But since human beings quite frequently prefer lots of things to do, this book will continue to guide you with action steps to take along your path.

When you take the time to write about your future, your life shifts itself to accommodate your expectations. Your expectations and intentions shape your results – every day. The powerful tool of getting clear about your intentions is good for you, and even better for everyone you meet.

Set Your Intention for Prospecting

Before you embark on prospecting activities, get clear on some great outcomes. This is an interesting practice, because you want to be clear on outcomes and also open to opportunities.

This may be a mental challenge: to anticipate great outcomes and also to feel relaxed and happy, trusting enough in the greater good of the universe, trusting that everything is going right; to be relaxed and happy even in the midst of wanting great outcomes.

So, before you pick up the phone, invite three new transactions, deals, clients or experiences to occur as a result of your actions. Picture a home sale closing (if you are a realtor) or imagine four new clients signing up (if you have a different product or service). What would be great? Set your intention for your communications for the day.

Even as I sit to write this book, I realize that while I am clear on my long-term intentions, and I write my vision and I know my intentions around my life – I may not have stopped to get extremely clear about what would be great. So one morning I thought about it and asked for four new coaching clients to show up.

A few days later, I received an e-mail from a former coaching client who wanted to sign up for four new sessions. Then, she brought two friends who also wanted coaching.

It may or may not be difficult to get clear about your intention, but it most certainly requires time and energy. When you live with intention, and you are clear about what you want, your life will flow with renewed energy. The wanting invites life force to flow into and through all of your actions. You have a purpose, and when you live with clarity about your purpose, everything is so much easier. Life keeps sending you new opportunities for you to grab and run with.

Now that we have talked about the big picture, and setting the vision and expectation for your next year, your next month and even your next week, understand the role intention plays in creating more from every opportunity. Get clear on your intention before picking up the phone. If you have an appointment, drive to the appointment with a sense of happy anticipation.

I have a funny (well, sort of funny) story about anticipation. It is winter 2006 and the real estate climate is getting chilly. I am selling houses. I receive a call from a man who needs to sell his house. I take the call to mean that he has decided I am the right realtor and I am going over to see the house almost as a formality — I am completely, 100 percent sure I have the sale. The home belongs to a woman I know and her husband; I know the family; and the daughter has babysat my children.

What I don't realize until I am in the listing meeting — I show up very relaxed with some information about recent sales in the neighborhood, but I don't show up with a formal presentation — is that he is meeting with me as a courtesy to his soon-to-be ex-wife, and his vision is to hire a male realtor who lives and works within a few miles of this home.

I walk in with complete confidence and begin to discuss how he can prepare his home for sale. He chooses to hire me and I sell the house.

I had no idea going in to that meeting that he was not expecting to hire me. He had a vision of a realtor and I was not that vision. My vision was that I would be the perfect person to sell the house, and that did occur. It was funny, though. Looking back I have clarity that my perfect certainty swung the deal. He did not actually end up interviewing the "competition," although before I walked in the door, he planned to do just that.

Your own certainty absolutely shifts the outcome of all of your experiences. When you pitch your idea, concept or product, know with certainty that it will work for the situation at hand. That certainty is so enjoyable, so warm, so attractive, and so incredibly tempting. Perfect certainty is a rarity. When you can bring this with you, it will prove irresistible.

One of my coaching clients, Stacy, began to shift into this place of being positive, staying focused on the positive outcomes her business would experience, and communicating certainty when presenting to clients. Here is what she says about working on getting clear and staying in a good frame of mind:

"I have become very aware of my own sense of self and now I am able to stop and think of what I am trying to convey and the right way to do it," says Stacy. "If I am allowing negative energy in, I stop right away and change it by reading something positive — usually regarding karma — to stop the negative from entering my space. Every day I vision what I want, business and personal. I have found things then come your way."

Service Orientation: Caring About the Client

To achieve the greatest results, it is not just about intention, nor just about being in a good mood or feeling happy. To rocket your results, move your motivation into a service orientation.

You may wish to accomplish a number of sales, and earn a number of dollars. Perhaps you are seeking a new job. These goals and intentions are going to fly home for you a lot faster when you ask "How Can I Be of Service?"

Stop for a moment and visualize whatever you are bringing to the planet to be fabulous. Allow your service to provide inspiration and success to the recipient. Let's take real estate. Your sale of their home will allow the client to move to his or her next place, or invest in his or her next investment. You are providing a service that has the capacity for joyous celebration when the sale is complete.

It is never really about just you. Although when you get this, and truly move into being a light for others, brightening the path for the client, then everyone wins, no one loses, and the great part is your sales results move up with the additional benefit of all of the people in the transaction feeling good at the same time.

One of my coaching clients was listening to the concept of picturing smooth transactions, easy closes of escrow, great people to work with, and easy sales, and asked if that was a self-centered approach? Wasn't she being selfish if she pictured these nice easy closes of escrow?

Then I asked the question, "Is the universe served if the buyer and seller are on track, everyone wants the same outcome, the escrow moves quickly to close and the desires of the seller (to sell quickly) and the buyer (to move in quickly) are all met?" Is it self-centered for an agent to consciously choose transactions that will operate in this manner? Or would it be actually beneficial for all involved?

Another client wanted to sell wonderful juice that has healing properties. When people drink the juice, it gives them more energy and decreases health problems. So when people sign up with her to sell more of the juice, the whole planet wins. This is the kind of "greater-good" thinking that shows a motivation with an altruistic component.

It is up to every individual to figure out his or her intention and to get clear on what he or she wishes to attract into his or her life.

When you are clear on great clients coming your way, a great new job showing up, or great sales flowing into your path, it actually serves everyone in your life. Understanding the concept of the world being served when you become true to your own greatness may free you to experience better results every day. This conscious attention to nurturing yourself is healthy and good for everyone in your world.

The discipline lies in staying clear on the intention, staying clear on the desired outcome, and then relaxing and going with the flow as you navigate the waters of the actual sale or transaction. When something happens that could be considered a setback, you may choose to see it a different way. Relax and know that it is all going to work for the best. That is the best feeling. When you trust the outcomes are always going to be right — no matter what the outcomes may be — you move into a whole new level of being.

What you will learn in this chapter:

· *What makes you happy is unique for you*
· *When you ask yourself to feel good, you can move into feeling good*
· *Be clear about your mindset before communicating with others*

CHAPTER 4

How to Get Into a Good Mood Before You Prospect

These steps are designed to trigger that thought or feeling that gives you a sense of supreme good will, excitement, confidence and joy.

When was the last time something you did gave you a shiver of excitement? When was the last time you felt profound gratitude? What causes you to feel an extreme sense of well-being?

People outside of you may not be able to accurately discern how it is that you move into the highest possible state of joy. You own your own feelings of happiness, and when you stay in your energetic flow, open to the love and peace and happiness that abounds, this flow is something whole and beautiful.

In Native American culture, there is a saying that you walk in beauty. This is being in tune with the environment and people around you. Begin taking time every day to put yourself in this place of being, feeling and knowing your life is already on track.

One of my wonderful students loves her life. At age 72, she is still discovering new ways to live her life. She recently moved into selling online travel and the excitement is catching. She called in distress one morning. "I am reading a book that tells me I have to get into joy. I just don't know what that is," she said. I asked her if she changes the word to comfort, peace or contentment, does that help? Then I reminded my lovely student that when she reads, she feels happy. When she gardens, planting flowers in her yard, this gives her a solid feeling of happiness. And travel really rings her bell. I know these things about her, of course, because she is someone I teach. You know these things about you, although sometimes this information can become buried and you have to dig it up into your present consciousness.

She was working so hard to find those things that make her feel joyful, she forgot that sometimes the small things in her life can bring a great deal of peace.

Cell Phone and E-Mail Distractions

In the landscape of our culture, it is very much a connect-now, speak-with-me-now, e-mail-me-now, and text-me-right-now-please culture. People hunger for the exciting new technology of hand-held products, so it becomes ever easier to communicate with each other, any time, any place.

Sales and business people often feel that success depends upon the immediacy of the answer. In real estate, as in many other sales professions, this is quite prevalent, with realtors carrying cell phones everywhere, wanting to always be available for the client.

To stay in a clear and positive state of being, answer the phone at the time you choose and return calls when you are ready and poised to do so. Stay focused on giving your undivided attention to the client. Answer when it is right, and hold off if for some reason it is not right to speak with that client or that person at any one specific time. Make a commitment to communicating when you are in a good place.

It really works. The world keeps turning on its axis, even if you are not present for your client 24 hours a day, seven days a week.

Here is an example of a home sale where the seller and his representative were available only when they wanted to be. In a $1.1 million home sale in February 2007 in the Willow Glen neighborhood of San Jose, California, the seller happened to be of Orthodox Jewish faith. From about 3 p.m. Fridays until Sundays each week there was to be no fax, phone or e-mail communication. Not a knock on the door, nor inspections, or business of any kind. The buyer did not want calls or business on Sundays, so business was off until Mondays.

Guess what? The deal closed on time, and no one had to work, answer questions or manage information regarding that deal Fridays through Sundays. There was a two- or three-day break every week. It all worked out and no one worked on this project for almost three days every week. The world kept turning.

I had another client who was deeply committed to building her online travel business. Her business depended on attracting team members to join up and sell online travel. She expressed fear of success, and believed success would take the form of answering the phone and being available 24 hours a day. As soon as she became clear that she was powerful enough to communicate when she would be available, perhaps one or two evenings a week and only one weekend day, she relaxed. Of course people will still conduct business with you, even if you only wish to be available at certain days and times. In fact, when you are very clear about your availability, then you will attract people for whom that availability is a match. So you don't have to worry about it.

When the phone rings or the text message appears, be in a state of awareness of your own energy. Here are some times not to answer the phone:

- When you are driving in traffic or feeling tense about driving in traffic
- When your children are yelling in the background

- When you woke up on the wrong side of the bed and feel extremely bummed out
- When something else just happened to you that you are worried or concerned about

Then, call or e-mail the person back when your energy is back to normal or better. Communicate when you have all of your attention on the person you are calling. Paying attention and communicating with a great level of conscious intent about your client will allow you to listen more clearly, understand better, and get things done more quickly when the person asks or wishes for something.

If you are almost always present when talking on the phone or e-mailing someone — and I mean present, energetically speaking — then you can gloss over this portion of the book quickly.

If you realize that you have been halfway present for many of your conversations — answering the phone when you are doing something else or thinking about someone else — then change may take some time. Awareness is the first step. You will reap stronger results when you are in the present and focused during each conversation.

When you communicate from a clear and conscious perspective, you can hear your clients' request with greater clarity. You have room also to explore opportunities that otherwise you may miss. You will be able to pick up on cues that you would miss if you managed the conversation without being fully present to it.

How to Improve Your State of Being and Smile When You Make the Communication

Here are some ideas to help you achieve tenfold your expectations on a daily basis:

- Be of good cheer before you answer the phone or an e-mail.

- Think about a great vacation that you plan to take, and begin to imagine how it will feel, right before you go in and answer e-mail messages.

- Be conscious of your thoughts and your intentions prior to any communication with anyone.

- Be in a place where you communicate non-verbal feelings of safety, security, confidence and joy.

When you are not feeling good, it's not good for anyone. Stop and write a list of times, places and experiences that put you into a state of happiness. Suggestions from my students:

1. Listen to a song you love. Play it loud.

2. Sing.

3. Find a CD that inspires you and listen to it.

4. Watch a movie that makes you feel good.

5. Think about a time you felt awesome. Ride a horse at a breakneck gallop up steep hills.

6. Imagine skiing with speed down the mountain on a clear sunny day.

7. Hold or cuddle children or loved ones.

8. Take your dog for a romp in the forest or park.

9. Play silly computer or video games.

10. Call someone who makes you smile.

11. Take a walk.

12. Read client testimonials thanking you for past successes (courtesy staging instructor).

13. Ride your bike.

14. Go to the gym and sweat out anything that doesn't feel good inside.

15. Play hoops on the blacktop (spoken like the true gym rat that I once was, nothing like hoops on the blacktop to feel good).

16. Read a book that you love over and over again.

17. Make some custom jewelry (suggested for my book editor who makes custom jewelry).

18. Go grocery shopping for luxury items.

19. Get your toes and nails done.

20. Go four-wheeling on bumpy dirt.

21. Daydream about all of the places you're going to go when your sales results burst into the stratosphere.

Please stop whatever you are doing right now, and make a personal list of 10 things you can do — that you *love* to do — that do not fail to put you in a great place emotionally.

This exercise is at the core of this book. And it is at the core of your ability to turn everything that *could* be an opportunity into an opportunity. So take a little time, and think about what you do that makes you feel good. When do you feel safe? When do you feel loved? When do you feel happy? Write down 10 things that you personally enjoy or things you have done that made you feel great.

Here is an example from my own distant past. In the late 1980s, I accepted a great writing job with the Sacramento Bee, a major metropolitan newspaper and part of the McClatchy chain of national newspapers. I was so excited! I made it to the Bee. This was my dream when I was going to college at the University of California at Davis, and I had planned to make it to the Sacramento Bee by age 30. When I got there at 26, I was blown away.

Here was the catch: I had to live in Yuba City, California. The year I moved to Yuba City, it ranked No. 329 out of the 329 places to live in a national survey. It didn't have a lot of resources then. A lot has changed. Then, Yuba City had fields, plum trees, rice paddies, some rivers, and very inexpensive housing. Raised in Palo Alto, California, I had always lived in an urban area, a hop and skip from San Francisco. Talk about a fish out of water.

As the Yuba City Bureau Chief (that was a title I gave myself; I think the Bee called me a news correspondent), my job was to travel around Yuba City, Marysville, Oroville, Chico, Nevada City, and Brownsville to gather breaking news information. I had nine cities and two counties and thousands of acres of agricultural land to cover. The area had the largest poverty rate in the state, and the greatest percentage of children living in poverty. The drug methamphetamine was becoming very popular.

This also was the first time I had ever worked outside of a news-room atmosphere. I had a home office for the first time. So I would wake up, look around, and try to get into a good place, and drive miles and miles in my Toyota pickup searching for news. The weather was about 110 degrees from about mid-June to September and I couldn't afford air conditioning.

Here is what I did. A movie theater complex was built in Yuba City that year. Joy! I would work from 8 a.m. to about 1 p.m. pounding the pavement for news. The movie "Big" with Tom Hanks had just come out. This was a hilarious movie! I would go see that movie several afternoons a week for $2 and laugh the whole time, and cry a little, and feel so happy. Then I would pop back to work on my tiny portable computer (this preceded laptops, it was a 15-pound small computer with a telephone modem to transmit articles), and write. The screen was 3" by 4" wide. Good thing I had good eyesight!

That was a wild time in my life. I am so appreciative of that movie theater. Before the Law of Attraction became prevalent in the national consciousness, I was already getting into a good place to maintain my sanity in that post. Luckily I was hired to write for the Santa Barbara News-Press after three years in Yuba City. Following three summers in 110-degree heat, I moved to a place where my home was two miles from the beach, with a gorgeous view and 72 degrees every day of the year. My salary doubled. It was a little bit easier then, to be in a good place.

The point is to always stay in a good place. When you cannot possibly feel good, don't prospect, don't make calls, hold off on making big decisions. Let it pass. Do things to feel better. Picture where you want to be, envision what would be great, or actually experience something wonderful. Eat a chocolate sundae! Or drive somewhere that makes you feel special.

This endless trek towards getting into a good place is your personal responsibility. Grab it, take it and run. Then watch how high you can fly.

Expanding This Concept Further

The title of this book is "*Prospect When You Are Happy*." What if you don't know if you ever will be perfectly happy? The concept around feeling good is to do what you can, when you can, to always move your own energy to a higher vibration.

Laughter is a very high vibration. Laughter, joy, relaxation, delight, happiness, fulfillment, exuberance, bounce-off-the-wall excitement — these all are expansive emotions that will allow you to break through into new levels of success. Getting into this feeling before you get everything you want is the key to getting everything you want.

Your success is limited only by your own thoughts, feelings, vibration, and the obstacles you have invited and allowed in your path.

And everything is relative. If you have made only two sales in two years and you wish to make 20 sales every month, this may take deep and true changes of feeling and vibration. Be kind to yourself as you move into the results you want. Know that you are on the way. You may want to seek more information, new teachers, new ideas and new ways you can move into where you wish to be in terms of results.

If you are already making 20 sales every month (or 20 new connections, or however you define your own success) and you wish to gently bump that up to 24 per month, you won't have to change your vibration as much.

Take a look at where you are, and where you want to go.

When you look at your life, are you conscious of how you focus your thoughts? How carefully do we plan and set our intentions for our interactions?

People who are in sales can move into a level of unconscious behavior. Once you have been on dozens and dozens of sales appointments, you can easily succumb to sleeplike dreamlike states where you are not actually listening to the client or customer.

This book is about moving into an intense, positive and aware state when you are prospecting, conducting sales conversations, job interviews, beaming your vision, your image of how you wish to be perceived. Listen to the person you are communicating with, and truly respond to what they want and need. Be in a good place yourself, and listen to the people in your life.

What happens when you are not listening? What happens when you are prospecting from rote sets of scripts without an infusion of excitement and vision? We'll take a look, in the next chapter.

What you will learn from this chapter:

• *When you stay the same, you risk missing out
on opportunities that will come to you only when
you lift your vibration*

• *If you are seriously despondent, you may need to seek
assistance beyond the cheer that this book can provide*

• *When you change, you can open yourself up to
better experiences than ever before*

CHAPTER 5

What Happens If You Don't Focus Intention and Prospect from a Good Place?

What do you risk if you do not embrace all that you know is possible? Do you risk staying in a financially deplorable lifestyle? Do you risk missing several vacations you might have taken? What will you miss out on?

This is your life. If remaining the same is what you truly want to experience, that's easy. Don't change. Stay the same. That is the path of least resistance. Staying the same is comfortable.

Staying the same is something that you know how to do. In fact, most of our physiology is dedicated to staying the same. We have internal set points: our weight, our income, our basic operating lifestyle. All of these set themselves to remain the same. To change, you consciously choose change, and step into change with commitment and dedication.

When you don't change, opportunities are knocking and you can't hear them. You are too busy feeling miserable, locked into memories of times when this didn't work or that didn't work. When you don't change, you may not achieve as much as quickly, and you are likely to miss cues that could have lifted your future into the stratosphere.

Remember: Your energy beams like a radio station.

Your radio waves will reach around the planet, or just across the street. Good energy? You will find others with great energy. Do you feel lousy, down, depressed or like you aren't worth much? Even animals have a way of knowing how you feel. People can sense your fear or your lack of confidence, and may be turned off by what you are giving out. If you are trying to achieve sales results, or life results, it may serve you to change your energy instead of wallowing in fear, depression or despair.

If you resonate with fear, depression or despair, you may need to seek help to change. It may not be something you can accomplish without professional assistance. Please seek help if you need it. How do you know if you need help? When it is suggested that help is available, is this something that resonates with you? You have a compass, an internal guide, and when you need help, and open to it, you may find that help is closer than you think. This book is not designed to provide professional help for people in a deep state of depression.

This book is about nudging people who are focused and committed on being in the positive to experience even greater change, and to accelerate the change they might already be experiencing. Should you find that you have trouble getting out of bed in the morning, please ask for help from people who are qualified to assist.

Regardless of how you get there, to the degree that you are able to lift yourself up — to change your own chemistry to feel good — this is the degree to which the results in your life will change. Change how you feel, and you change how people will view you.

Here is an experiment. Go out and say something really rotten in line at the coffee shop. Say something totally depressing. Watch people give you lots of space and stand as far away from you as possible.

Now, go into another coffee shop, or a grocery store, beaming light. Bounce off the wall with happiness. See what happens now. Everyone wants part of that energy. You can attract or push people away with how you approach every waking moment. It's your choice, it's your life. Be someone you would like to get to know, or don't. Be a grump. Don't change. Your call; your life!

The tools to change are all around you, in books, in classes, in messages from co-workers, and from professionals. When you are ready, the teacher will appear. Take in what you wish so you can become everything you have wanted to become. This is your life. In the chapters ahead, discover more tools to attract all of the success you wish to attract into your life.

What you will learn from this chapter:
- *Appreciation is a glorious magnet for great things in your life*
- *Appreciate every person and experience in some way; this releases resistance to the learning*

CHAPTER 6

Be Appreciative

Appreciate everyone, appreciate everything. Give your life permission to make you happy. Give everything that succeeds a victory yell.

Make conscious effort every day to see things in appreciative light. One client calls. One new good thing occurs. Stop and go crazy about it. Really celebrate. On your next five phone calls for the day, mention "I'm in a great mood because something good just happened."

So many individuals criticize themselves all day long. Something wonderful will occur and then you find yourself stuck in traffic. When you arrive at your appointment, what are you thinking about? Are you deep in appreciation for the appointment?

It is easier to fall into the game where you believe everything is wrong, and easier to believe that nothing is enough. I have a lovely student, a realtor, who is a buyer magnet. She believes, however, that she will not make it in real estate until she has listing agreements and seller-side deals in hand. So she is making it big, closing deal after deal after deal, pleasing many happy buyers, and she cannot stop and think about her own grace and business prowess.

Look how crazily our minds operate. No matter what we do, we at times allow the inner critic to jump in and say how badly we are doing. We don't always stop and take our milestones and celebrate them.

When you stop, recognize the beauty in your life, when you give appreciation, you will find more joy, more beauty, more appreciation than ever before.

Appreciate Each Call or Communication

When you are on the phone or in a meeting with a potential client, or someone with whom you already work, express appreciation. Find one thing to single out and appreciate with every single person in every situation.

Focus your attention on what is good, what is right, and what is working. Be completely honest and true when you express your appreciation.

Trust your instinct. You never know when the most amazing opportunity of your life may fly in and land in your lap. Expressing appreciation sets into motion powerful and positive vibrations, feelings and experiences. Being appreciative sets you apart.

Be appreciative also when someone does not choose you, too.

What?

Yes, express appreciation when the sale doesn't go or the transaction doesn't fly. Find a way to feel trust in the universe. Be committed to the next thing showing up. When a sticky deal doesn't go through, moving it off your plate will allow space for new, easier, more wonderful deals to appear. You may feel a sense of loss. That's being honest. Then open your heart to allow more, new, better, more wonderful and exciting opportunities in that space.

Appreciation decreases resistance. In the summer of 2007 I was fortunate to sell a home quickly despite a sluggish real estate market climate. I expressed great appreciation to the seller throughout the entire experience. The seller was a person whose viewpoint was a "what could go wrong" viewpoint. The questions asked were focused on what and how things could go wrong. As I was focused on being in a good place, and expressing appreciation, I continued to stay focused on appreciating the buyer (the home sold in six days) and appreciating everything the seller did to ready the home for the quick sale. I communicated appreciation at all times during the escrow process. Things could easily have blown up with that particular sale because the lending climate had turned treacherous for the buyer, who had a small down payment. By focusing on the good at all times, this transaction went through. It easily could have failed. To express appreciation is to keep the "eyes on the prize." It is a discipline that will reap many rewards.

As you focus on appreciation, more of those good things will become true for you. As you change your world to become more in alignment with your highest good, you may find some lag time as your reality shifts to reflect your new outlook. Appreciation of the small things is like grease to ease the changes and speed your transition. This is also the key to attracting the perfect clients, the next topic of conversation.

What you will learn in this chapter:

- *Getting clear on your perfect client attracts great clients to you like a magnet*
- *Taking time to imagine your ideal client moves you a step above the rest*

CHAPTER 7

Attracting the Perfect Client

Who is your perfect client? What does he or she value? How much money does he or she want to spend? Where does your client go on vacation? How easy is it for your client to make a decision?

As you clarify your vision of your perfect client, you set an intention for these people to find you. You stop and invite perfect clients into your life. You do not have to figure out how they will find you.

When you become very clear on something that you want, isn't it easier to find it? Let's say you want a new computer. How much do you want to spend? What does it need to do? How much memory do you need? How fast should it operate? Does it need to be networked to other computers or your printer? If you are not specific, you know the wide range of products that can come in the door. When you become very clear — your next home, your next car, your next vacation, your next pet — the right choices will come to you in a much easier fashion. You will find it easier to recognize the right choices because you are clear on what you want.

Think about buying a home. If you are helping someone buy a home who doesn't know what he or she wants, you will have to expend a tremendous amount of energy. You show the client every house under the sun. This quickly exhausts your energy and the client's energy as well. He or she will become so tired of looking at the "wrong" thing that he or she may give up.

Now think about helping a family who knows what they want. This family has chosen the neighborhood, the price range, the look and the feel of the home in question. The family decides they want lots of windows, a vaulted entryway, a price range that can work, and they even tell you the schools they wish the children to attend.

The realtor will quickly narrow the search, show four or five homes, write a contract and close escrow. The family knows what they want, and everyone wins.

When you know what you want, the universe can serve you with ease.

When you know what you want, then you can be given what you want. And you can want even more then, and achieve clarity on new things. The cycle keeps going.

Who is your perfect client? Is he or she someone who:

- needs your product or service
- will refer your business to many clients a lot like them
- makes decisions easily
- pays for your service on time and with ease
- is friendly and easy to work with
- communicates clearly and lets you know how you can help them

Please stop everything you are doing now and grab a pencil or pen.

Write a list of your perfect client attributes. Don't worry if you are busy, or if you are not sure really why you need to list what is perfect. You are most likely able to come up with a dozen reasons to not do this right this moment, but do it anyway. Stop and list what would be incredible, awesome, inspiring and true in your favorite customers. What do you want to see? Picture it now.

Are you done yet? No, not yet!

Now that you have a list of at least 10 attributes of your perfect client, let's take this a step further. Picture feelings of excitement, joy, and nirvana and delight when this person or people come into your life. Picture yourself knowing with certainty that you are meeting all of the right people, all of your perfect clients, right now. Imagine these clients were always around you and you could not see them before.

One of my students is an online travel network marketing business owner. She is actively involved in hosting booths at events every few weeks. She became clear on her perfect clients, and opened up to finding them all over the place (not just at her booth during events). She was taking her pup to doggie day care, and another woman noticed a travel flyer in my student's hands. These two women have seen each other for months and never knew that enthusiasm about travel was something they have in common. As network marketing relies on "team building" for success, the student was delighted to meet a potential travel business team member at the doggie day care.

Desire coupled with emotion is stronger than desire alone. Saying or writing words around your desires is an excellent beginning. The next step is to get ramped up emotionally about that result flying into your life.

Then take this daydream a step further.

Picture your perfect client (you know, the one who personifies the list of attributes you have already written). Picture your perfect client bringing you seven more perfect clients. Now you have EIGHT PERFECT CLIENTS or customers. Picture them all wrapping up the purchase or taking advantage of the services you are providing. Picture this smoothly flowing into your life.

Now, picture the results, the cash flow, the freedom and everything else you have wanted to flow in to your life. Stop and be the person who already has this working perfectly in your life. See yourself as the person who now is telling your friends and co-workers how to attract their perfect clients. Contribute to those who don't understand how this all works yet, by teaching them how to attract wonderful clients and experience amazing business results.

Keep ratcheting up what you want, and keep seeing it done. Then let it all go. Let go of everything you want. Relax about the results.

What you will learn in this chapter:

• *After you are clear on what you want, and desire it with emotional intensity, let it go*

• *Allow yourself to say no when opportunities are not in alignment with your vision*

CHAPTER 8

How to Let It Go and When to Say No

Let it go? Wait! How could we suggest that letting go of what you want, that intention, that desire, when just moments ago we suggested you grab on to your intentions with all of your might?

It is all true. When you become clear on what you want, and become happy about it, beam the energy of that vision like radio waves from a tower. Your communications will beget amazing results.

Getting clear on what you want is a great step toward achieving your goals and getting the results that you seek. Moving towards your goals with an attitude of service, wellness, delight, joy, enthusiasm, clarity and happiness is like having a tank of gas and making sure the oil gauge shows "full" and the oil is clean, too.

And yet, even with all of this in place, the greater truth is that if you are able to be detached about the outcome at the same time — even when you have an intention, and you are emotional and passionate about wanting the outcome —the floodgates will open and your results will swim at you at breakneck speed.

Here is a personal example. In the summer of 2006, I put together a list of everything I wanted to have happen in my life. I wanted more income, all of my mortgages paid off, my writing to take flight, books written and published, selling well, children happy and doing well in school, my husband feeling happy. Then I just threw on the list "40 acres to play, within two hours of home." The income wishes were steep. I let my mind float on each of the things I wanted passionately for myself, and the 40 acres to play I threw in for fun and for the benefit of my husband.

We live in the heart of Silicon Valley, where home lots are measured in square feet as opposed to acres (my friends in Tennessee laugh at that), and one acre can be $1 million. A half-acre lot within an hour of Silicon Valley would typically be in the $400,000 to $700,000 range, depending on the proximity to good schools. So 40 acres to play sounds relatively expensive.

Every day for four months, I included this wish in my list. In January 2007, we bought 37.8 acres of land in the Santa Cruz Mountains for less than $200,000. It does not seem possible, and looking back, I know how lucky we are. Lucky? Or did the universe work to bring us this land so our family can play? When we were visiting the property, I asked for a sign from the universe. The song that blasted from the one clear radio station was "Ripple," a Grateful Dead song that my husband and I have always loved — it was the first song played at our wedding. Then the next song that played was an Allison Kraus song that my cousin sang at our wedding. Now, that felt good. We closed escrow and it was so easy.

If I had not listed that "40 acres to play" on the wish list, would I have scrolled through vacant land offerings online? It is more likely that if the wish were not on my list that I would not believe we could afford 40 acres. If, when we called the listing agent, and he assured us that we would not like that land, would we have persisted in going to see it? It was funny how it all played out, and I know with certainty that owning that land is a financial decision that will serve us well, a great investment for our children, and a great asset to the family well-being. We now possess our own park and camping ground with no reservations needed, far into the future.

So, prospect when you are happy, picture the

That was about how to let go. Letting go of being attached to your desires is a great way to speed up the manifestation of that wish.

perfect clients, imagine everything you want to occur in your life, imagine all of your results and then let them go.

What You Want and What You Get May Look Differently Than You Expect

Here's why not being attached is such a great tool. You ask for what you want, and what you receive still may surprise you. You ask for a perfect client. Soon after that time, you run into someone in the grocery store who needs your services. However, this person is already booked with another service provider. Here is a true story that illustrates how life can give you what you want; and yet, in order to experience the fruition of the opportunity, you have to be open to it appearing and possibly feeling differently than you imagined.

I was teaching classes on how to get what you want, and I was encouraging students who were in real estate at the time to picture "come get me" listings. A "come get me" listing is when someone calls you and says essentially "can you come over and sell my house?" Realtors love these calls, it is usually a referral or someone they already know and like. One student asked "What is a 'come get me' listing? I don't understand." So we went into a meditation where the students all pictured someone calling out of the blue and asking them to list their home for sale.

That student e-mailed me two hours after the class ended. She went to lunch with a potential buyer, and he said to her, "Will you list and sell my home in Modesto?" She was able to experience the essence of a 'come get me' listing, in person.

So I was reflecting on the good fortune of my students, and I thought to myself how much I would enjoy a "come get me" listing call myself, for a nice financial summer pick-me-up. I quietly pictured someone calling and asking me to list their home, and then let it go.

The next morning, the phone rang. It was a woman from my daughter's school, and I didn't remember that she had my telephone number. "Who is this again?" I asked. I'll call her CT. CT asked me some questions, and quickly I understood that she wasn't happy with her current realtor and was fishing for answers on how to sell her home. We began to talk, but I quickly steered her away from considering *me* as her realtor! I didn't want the headaches. She already had a realtor! Then I paused.

I reflected.

What had I asked for the morning before? What had I pictured? But I had not pictured this exact scenario. I pretty much tried to push the "come get me" listing opportunity away, because I did not recognize it.

Luckily, the universe has a sense of humor, and Law of Attraction is absolute. It always works, and it works all the time.

Later that day while my children were in preschool and I detoured for an unexpected grocery stop, I am walking in to the store with my grocery cart. Guess who is shopping right in front of me? You guessed it. CT. She stops and says "Oh, I am so happy to see you! My husband and I really want you to sell our house."

I realize in that moment that my resistance is silly and that my mental picture of a "come get me" listing and the true experience of a "come get me" listing were not identical. Yet the result was the same. I am able to sell this home easily, and I love and respect the clients.

When Do You Say No?

You are pitching your product or service. You are excited and happy about the conversation. Your vision for the outcome is clear. And you are clear that how it unfolds may be different than you expect. When do you let go? When do you turn down an opportunity or decline working with someone who might want your product or services?

Be of absolute security in your own ability to discern right from wrong, good from bad, tall from short and lost from found. What is good? What is bad? When you are speaking with someone, how do you feel?

You don't have to say no to an opportunity, but if you do happen upon a conversation that feels truly awful, give yourself permission to say no. Prospect with happiness, and focus your energy where it may have the potential to grow.

Trust your inner knowing. Trust that small voice of inspiration. Trust the contrast between going with the flow and walking up a steep hill where the backs of your calves are in agony and you can't catch your breath. Going against the current will feel different from swimming with the flow.

When you are going against the current, the communication with a potential client will not feel the same as when things are working. When things are working, you can expect:

- Synchronicity
- Coincidences in your favor (referring back to the "come-get-me" listing call from CT, when she gave me her work number I discovered we had both worked for the same company at one time; this helped me understand and serve her even better)
- To call people at the right time when they want to talk to you
- Easy referrals where the client recommends you to other people who need your products or services
- A sense of mutual respect and understanding
- A surge of energy that comes through when people are working together for the common good

When you are going against the grain, climbing a steep hill, battling the elements along the way, things may feel more like this:

- The potential client avoids calls or does not call back
- The person is rude or short with you
- The person asks you to never call them again

· It is never the right time when you contact them

When things don't feel right, you can do some things to change the chemistry of an interaction. Or you can walk away.

Walking away from a situation when your energy is not the best fit provides great side-effects. Here are some reasons to say no to the wrong job, the wrong opportunity, the wrong client or the wrong customer:

· When you push against people, customers, potential opportunities that are hard work and are not any fun, you may find that this tone is set for the length of the relationship

· You may find it takes more energy and you receive less money for the work or the opportunity

· The lessons you learn may trigger the thinking "I knew better than to work with someone who acted like that"

· When you go against your gut feeling, you may find yourself working for less than you are worth

· You may not experience referrals or easy connections to your next steps, as behind the communication is a level of angst or discomfort

Fortunately, life begins anew every day. As you infuse new consciousness into your day, you may navigate the old and invite the new. Keep doing what you are doing, and begin to sort for "the flow." Begin to get clear on when things are working well, and how to say yes to things that may feel uncomfortable, but not bad, and opportunities that feel new and exciting. Say yes to a lot of new opportunities!

Also, recognize when something is *not* working, and permit yourself to cut your losses and move your energy where it can flourish. It is like when a plant won't take root because the sun isn't bright or the water isn't right. You don't think twice about moving the plant to a place where it will flourish. Allow yourself to move to situations where your ideas will flourish, too.

Prepare yourself now for your life to work like it has never worked before. As you become clear on your intent, infuse intention and focus into your prospecting activities, opportunities flow into your life. Then, get ready to make "The Close."

What you will learn from this chapter:
· *To get clear on closing*
· *To ask for closes*
· *To be interested in closes*
· *How the focus on the close begets more closes*

CHAPTER 9

Vision the Close

It is 1993, and I have a job interview with a high-tech company that makes chips. Not the potato kind. I was working for a small public television station, earning little and writing a lot. Duct tape covered patches of carpet where the old carpet was worn through. For the job interview, I walk into a fabulous, glassy, modern, multi-million dollar setting and the words of my brother are ringing in my ears. "Don't forget to ask them when you start. Just say when can I start?" Talk about going for the close.

This calmed my nerves and I did start, not too long after the interview. My job was writing articles about good works, and helping the company make donations to schools. It was a dream job with great pay, great people and a great working environment.

When you pick up the phone to speak with a client or customer, remember to remind them about the close. Be clear on the potential close. What will this look like? What will this feel like? Lead the client or potential customer to also be clear about the close, when your product or service has done its job, has served them well, and you are done.

It is 2007 and the housing market is jumping around, and prices are declining in many neighborhoods. In one neighborhood where I have a listing appointment, there are 148 homes for sale in a 4-mile radius. When I land the listing, I bring the "Sold" rider (a 6-inch by 18-inch sign that rides on top of the yard sign in front of the house when the home is sold). The seller places it in her bedroom where she can look at it every day. We sell the home against odds in six days. She is picturing "Sold" every day. This is working.

Picture the close. Feel good about the close. Some people get very interested and drawn in to the very opposite. The Law of Attraction will bring you more of what you focus on, think about, and believe in. So, where do you want your thoughts? What would you like to experience?

The discipline of believing in the close will serve you well. Describe the close to everyone you come into contact with — describe yourself as someone who closes deals. Or use the words you like. Begin to explain yourself in your own terms.

One student was struggling with adding people to her "down line" in a network marketing program. I will call her JT. She was selling an online system with a lot of enthusiasm. "I have figured it out," she said. "I need to add 1,200 people and I can retire. I need 27 people to sign up under me right away."

What if JT talks and thinks about the opportunity in a different way? The way she described the "need" to have 27 people sign up, it sounded like a weight on her shoulders and a problem that she was concerned about. In fact, when she talked about the experience of bringing 1,200 people on board, it sounded nearly impossible.

I suggest to JT that she focus on the opportunity as a gift she is giving. "Why not think about it like this," I suggested. "You have this amazing gift, where people can sell travel online, add a link and travel enthusiasm to their e-mail communication, and take trips and go fun places all while income is generated?" How does that feel? How does that sound?

A light went on for JT. She couldn't believe how much better it felt to give a gift of income generation tools, and share her love of travel with everyone she met. That felt so much better than focusing on how many people she *had to have in her down line* or the world would not keep turning on its axis.

So picture the close. The caviat is to picture the close serving every person involved. Picture it working for everyone. So the close works, and it works for everyone. If that *still* isn't working, picture the close differently. Infuse into your picture of the close a spirit of service.

When you are in service, and your product or gift to others is helping them where they already wish to go, then you move into the flow. Everything unfolds with less stress and more joy. You move into this way of being where *click, click, click* is the sound of your wishes and dreams falling into place. Life becomes more fun, more exciting, and you are able to renew your own zest for being alive on the planet in this day and time. One of the people I know who teaches meditation calls this being connected to source energy.

A student asked recently why she was not able to close a deal with a client. She was focused on bringing this person into her network marketing program. The client showed a lot of interest and appeared to want to sign up. Then she did not sign up on one given day. I suggested that my student relax, and allow her potential client to sign up when it is right for that client. Expect the close, and also allow everyone to go their own way. Keep focusing on attracting clients who will want to close. Any one client may or may not want to sign up. Yet by keeping your focus on attracting people who will close with you, that is what you will begin to experience. Near misses are a good sign that you are on track.

Appreciate the person who almost closes with you, and know that the close could be right around the next corner. Be certain about it. Be happy about it. Know it. The universe cannot withhold what you want when your focus is clear, the intent is clear, your actions are with certainty and peace of mind. Be at peace regardless of the outcomes. When you know you will have closes, you are a closer. Be a closer and more people will show up who will close with you. It is inevitable.

What you will learn in this chapter:
· *To accept easy opportunities*
· *To be on the look out for opportunities around every corner*
· *Going for the easy doesn't mean don't work hard*

CHAPTER 10

Go for the Easy

I recall one morning, when I worked for a 100,000-employee company, being in a large amphitheatre-style room, where an executive whom I admire was giving suggestions for business strategies. Everything was managed by quarter, so time was described as Q1, Q2, Q3, Q4 (you get the picture). "In Q2 we want you to go for the low-hanging fruit," he said. "You know, call the people you already know, the places where business opportunities are ripe and you have not picked them yet."

I can't remember why this was the focus; personally I always like to go for the three-point shot in basketball. For those not sports oriented, that's when you throw the ball from way outside the foul line and when it swishes through the net — oh, the joy!! The low-hanging fruit has never much appealed to me.

Now, if you always go for the easy, you may jump ahead to the next chapter. If this is something that you may forget or neglect to do, then hang out and determine if this rings true as a path you might embrace.

When you go for the easy transaction or business opportunity, you are going where there is a sense of "fit" already in place. Here is an example of an easy opportunity. Let's say you sell credit card services (merchant services). One night you order a pizza from your favorite pizzeria. You ask "Will you accept my debit card or my Visa?" The pizza owner says, "No, we only accept cash or checks."

An easy step would be to offer that pizzeria information about processing debit cards and credit cards to maximize his or her business results — and at the same time making a sale for you.

So often we sleep through hints and opportunities that are waiting for us, beaming at us, wanting to jump over large fences to get to us. We may not be listening with ears that can hear.

Always be on the look out for opportunities.

Clear your mind frequently.

Always wonder who might call and how connecting with that person in a mutually beneficial way may be of service to the planet.

Get clear about how you can provide opportunities for others, and allow others to bring you opportunities.

In the practice of deliberately invoking the Law of Attraction, focus on allowing good things to happen. Picture what you want, and allow opportunities into your life. Consciously stop and believe that good things will happen, expect good things to happen and then experience good things.

Before you make a call, before you go about your day, imagine all kinds of opportunities coming to you in ways you have never before experienced.

Here is an example of a real estate opportunity. It is summer of 2007 and I am tired of my cell phone. Tired of it ringing, tired of that feeling of needing to be near it, and tired of having it on. I am even tired of the ring tone. I ask the universe for an opportunity that does not come to me through the cell phone.

A few days go by.

I drive up to the place where my horse is boarded, and a man rides by on a horse. "CG needs to sell her house," he says. "She needs someone ethical to help her." Suddenly I have a real estate opportunity.

All it took was asking. Awesome! Life is so amazing. Get clear on amazing outcomes and you pave the way for everything good to flow into your life.

Go for the easy does necessarily not mean walking away when something goes wrong. Going for the easy doesn't mean "don't work hard." Go for the easy means that while you are getting happy about your life, be open to opportunities flowing in all that is around you, all the time. Life is so much fun when you open your heart to opportunities.

Stop looking so hard. Look easy. Be open.

What you will learn from this chapter:

• *To open your heart to an even bigger vision for yourself*

• *To go for the easy, then expect even better to occur*

CHAPTER 11

Expect More

Who is served when you stay small? No one. All are served when you stand tall. Be your brightest, most successful self and connect to your amazing future.

The only person who is standing in the way of you becoming every-thing you dream up is *you*. The mind limits, sifting through millions of cues and memories and thoughts that are all designed to maintain our status quo.

In order to change and shift into experiencing inspiring results every day, begin to see yourself in a new way. Begin to expect every action to lead to stronger results; you also may find that you begin to inspire others just by being around them.

When you commit to experiencing great results from all of your communications, you shine brightly and stand tall.

This journey into expecting more results will shift and alter the very fabric of your being. See your life bigger, brighter, and as you might wish it for someone you love. With crystal clarity, I can picture myself in Santa Barbara in 1990. I was mired in credit card debt. Every call was a debtor seeking payment. My mom gave me the greatest advice. She said pretend I am my older sister (I don't have a sister). Look at myself with the compassion a mother or older sister sees. Pretend I am my older sister, looking at someone who has some things to learn. My mom helped put me onto payment plans that I could afford with all of the credit card companies. Within a year, the debt was all clear.

See your life unfold with great leaps into the next chapter. Then stand in awe at the smallest successes. Feel gratitude when one tiny thing works right. Look for signs that will show you that are on your way to becoming and experiencing everything you want in your life.

You can always find signs that say everything is not working. The discipline that will provide steady breakthroughs, time after time, is focusing on everything that is working — and experiencing joy on the walk that you walk right now.

Let's say you are focused on selling houses. Think about what would give you joy. Take what you want and then double it, triple it or see it unfolding with 10 times the results you originally imagined.

For instance, let's say you wanted to sell 10 houses. Now see that as 10 houses worth over $1 million. Or 10 houses with 10 acres for each house. Or 25 houses in one year. Whatever you can do that will be outstanding for you. If you're in Texas, you may want to sell more than that. If you are in San Francisco, it could be your dream to sell seven houses in one year. Your dream is yours to choose, to follow, to believe, to focus upon.

Once you are clear about what would be great in your life, start to expect it. Have a chat with your brain. Tell it that these connections are happening, and to expect this and more. Have a conversation with yourself a month from now. Look back upon this present and laugh at how easy it became to live the intentions you set forth.

Then come back to the present and as you go through your day, allow your eyes to twinkle and your smile to come easily. After all, you know that everything is going to work, and you are confident the connections will happen out of this feeling of great certainty and happiness.

This is a creative state from which all prospecting will bear more fruit. When you expect wonderful things to occur, you emit amazing vibrations that others will find attractive.

It is easy to make the mistake of not dreaming big enough. When you set your sights too small, then you are not going to be asking the questions that will take you into the big wins. You might not see opportunities if these are not pathways you are ready to walk upon.

Setting the sights amazingly high will take you into a sweet place of being, will bring the feelings of certainty and joy to you; and may change the very neuronal patterns that connect your brain. You are changing the pathways so that you may experience all the joy you want in your life.

Expect more.

Take 10 things you want to happen, and write them down. Now gently shift them and look at what would be even better.

Here is an example. Let's say you sell chocolate online. You host a party for chocolate lovers. Let's say you really want at least one person to sign up with you to sell chocolate. What would be better? Picture a party where a dozen people all cannot wait to jump on to your healthy chocolate sales program. Picture them wanting the information, finding out about you and the business opportunity. Picture them burning to work in this profession — and they are so happy they found you.

Now, when you go about your day with that mental image, you will be attractive to people who are interested in healthy chocolate. You might kick up a conversation about healthy chocolate in the grocery store. You might buy a pin to wear that says "Ask Me About Healthy Chocolate."

What if everyone you helped was able to earn thousands of extra dollars every month? How would that feel? Picture yourself taking a great trip to somewhere warm, sunny and bright. Now invite 10 friends to travel with you. Or imagine something even better.

The only limits we place on our lives are placed by our own experiences shaping our desires, wishes and beliefs.

The forces that battle change will rise up when you launch this new way of approaching your life, or when you commit anew to this way of being: when you expect great things to happen every day.

Roll up your sleeves and ask for inspiration to break through your own barriers. We all have barriers — thought patterns that do not serve us, unconscious blocks that are buried deep within. The blocks may stem from years of parental or other influential messages. Are you ready to release your blocks? Commit to experiencing more from all of your communication. Allow yourself to learn whatever you need to learn, to move up into the place of experiencing more from every aspect of your life. Whatever you need to do to earn more money, feel better, love more deeply, whatever you seek to experience in your life — invite that in and allow inspiration to guide you to the right choices to make your dreams happen.

Get clear on your vision. When you are clear on your intentions, dream the vision again. When you dream the vision again, add emotion, images, sounds, colors, pictures, feelings, good smells. See if you can vision with every possible corner of your brain. The last chapter is coming upon us — and it is all about vision.

What you will learn from this chapter:

· *A vision is an insight into where you want to be in the future*

· *Your vision is constantly growing, changing and emerging*

CHAPTER 12

Vision

People who change, grow and become powerful guides of their own experience have this in common: vision. A strong vision is a guiding tool that will bring light and help you through the moments when you are not feeling powerful or creative.

Each and every day, wake to the knowledge that you are on your path. You are making the right choices. Find seeds of contentment wherever you look.

The key to success is waking every day with a renewed commitment to your vision. What if you don't have a vision? What is a vision? Isn't a vision for CEOs to build companies, not for regular people?

A vision can be easy. You can have a vision that spans five years, two years, one year, six months, three months, two weeks. It doesn't have to be a huge production that you have fear around (Will you get there? What if you don't? What if you need to change your vision?). Let go of the fear. Here is one way to create your vision.

Stop and write a holiday letter to yourself, dated a year or so from now. Pretend everything awesome has occurred. Write as though everything you wanted already happened. You know the holiday letters you receive? *"In March, Tom and I took the kids to Australia and we played with koalas. Then Courtney graduated from kindergarten with honors. Well, honors meaning she can write the entire alphabet. It's so exciting! In July we bought a time share in Hawaii and we are busy planning our first trip as we speak. I was able to land the new job and the kitchen remodel is complete. We had a great year! Wishing you all the best in the years to come."*

That's the kind of letter I am talking about. Your vision can be a snapshot of you one year from today. And you can change it when things begin to flow to you that are better than you even imagined. Clearly imagine the vision of you and your family a year from now.

Create a picture of yourself in the future. Imagine what you would like to see. Who is around you? What are you looking at? Are you looking at the ocean? What are you driving? Do you live in the home of your dreams?

Create an image of yourself in the vision for your future. Then, begin to imagine the feelings you have experienced in that place of success.

To heighten the pace at which you land in your vision:

- Be focused on allowing your vision to happen.
- Get clear on what "it" would feel like, look like and sound like.
- Be of solid good cheer as you embark on this trek. Be ever content even when things don't appear to be unfolding "right." Change how you look at every experience. Accept everything as being right.
- Connect with like minds. Find mastermind partners to support your journey.
- As you approach each day, act and behave as though you already have everything that you want.
- Beam light, smile before you prospect or communicate with others (that's what this whole book is about!).
- Let go when you want to sell something to someone and he or she decides it is not the right time or the right product or service.
- Let go of your entire vision at least once every day, asking something better to show up. Vision it; let it go, then vision it again.
- Be open to opportunities that may look and feel differently than you expected.
- Be certain that every call or communication could lead to something great.

- Be certain that something great is around every corner.

- Become crazy happy when something good does occur. Overflow with gratitude every day for the smallest victories.

- Step into the you that you want to be. Stop seeing that "you" as someone else. Become the you in your vision.

This is only a beginning. As you achieve more sales, more victories, more fruitful connections and more of what you are wanting, you will find new dreams to dream. This journey is exciting. What is so wonderful is that you *can* achieve your dreams.

Prospect when you are happy. It works.

Acknowledgements

My husband Randy gave me complete and total commitment to the creation of "Prospect When You are Happy," playing with our children Isabel, Paul and Madeline so I could find space and time to write. I am thankful for his love and complete faith in me. I thank Isabel, Paul and Madeline for the light they bring. My horse Dakotah gave me inspiration without which this book could not exist. My dad, Bob Glessing, is a great writer and published author. I thank my dad for his wry sense of humor. My brother Gerry gave me support, encouragement and taught me what I really needed to know to succeed. My mom is smiling from Heaven as I am writing each day.

Nancy Cleary was the most amazing publisher, jacket designer and supporter and immediately understood what I wanted to do with the book. Terri Hunter-Davis edited and I am not easy to edit. Thank you, Terri.

Michelle Humphries introduced me to effortless prosperity in the year 2002. The books of Sonaya Raman influenced me in the 1980s. Thach Nguyen taught Law of Attraction on a small CD he created. I bought the CD in the summer of 2006. I googled Thach and found him in cyberspace. He invited me to hang out with Matthew Ferry, Steven Sadleir and himself at a meditation retreat in Big Bear, California in October 2006. Three days of meditating with about 150 realtors inspired me to leave real estate, and turn to what I love: coaching, teaching and writing. Thanks to Thach, Matthew and Steven, I went back to doing what I love.

Thach and Matthew quite often direct people to the work of Abraham-Hicks. I love the messages from Abraham and see synchronicity in the messages that I am getting from source.

I have a personal coach, Celeste Hamman. She stuck with me during the bumps of this transition. Walter Zajac, psychic Walter, gently suggested I stay with writing when I went through financial breakdown en route to creating the new paradigm for my life. I have students and I can't name them all. All of you inspire me! Stacy, Maria, Paula, Joan, Joanne, Sonia, Janine, Sharon and Cindan, you are some of the people who gave me a great playground to create.

*For information on how you can get published
through the empowering imprint program at Wyatt-MacKenzie
visit www.wymacpublishing.com*

Wyatt-MacKenzie Publishing, Inc.
DEADWOOD, OREGON

www.ingramcontent.com/pod-product-compliance
Lightning Source LLC
Chambersburg PA
CBHW060627210326
41520CB00010B/1497